WHO MAKES? THE RULES?

Types of Government

Zephyr

Archway Publishing books may be ordered through booksellers or by contacting:

Archway Publishing
1663 Liberty Drive
Bloomington, IN 47403
www.archwaypublishing.com
1 (888) 242-5904

Interior Graphics/Art Credit: Zafar Chaudhry

ISBN: 978-1-4808-8043-6 (sc)
ISBN: 978-1-4808-8042-9 (e)

Print information available on the last page.

Archway Publishing rev. date: 07/26/2019

WHO MAKES THE RULES?

Types of Government

Written & Illustrated by
Zephyr

Zephyr was very upset. His parents had no idea how difficult it was for him to follow so many rules. He had to follow rules about bedtime and wake-up time. There were rules to do chores and keep his room tidy. Now he had to follow rules about how many pets he could have.

Zephyr had to a find a better way to run his family.

ANARCHY

Government has lost its power.
Lawlessness, violence, disorder will rule.

Hello Mr. Grasshopper

I need to find a new way
to make family rules.
How do you make the rules in your family?

What rules?
I live without rules.
I sing and dance when I want.
It does get a little tough during the cold winter months.
That's Anarchy.

MONARCHY

Absolute Monarchy: Government where one person rules.
Power passed down from one generation to the next.

Hello Queen Bee,

How do you make the
rules in your family?

Now let me think!
We have a queen who
controls everything we do.
That is "Absolute Monarchy."

MONARCHY

Constitutional Monarchy: One person is head of state. His/her power is limited by a constitution. Power is with elected officials.

Hello Queen Ant

How do you make
the rules in your family?

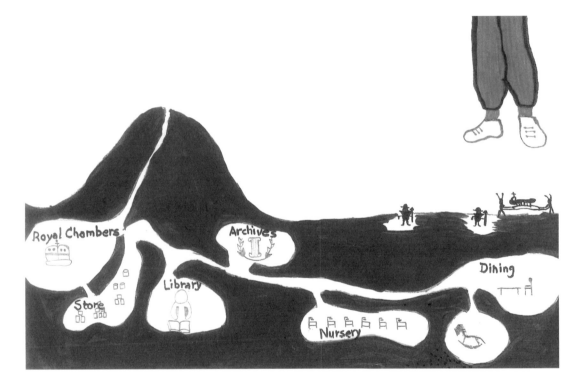

We have the better of the two
worlds. I am the "Queen" and I enjoy it.
We have rules that help the
subject stay happy and organized.
That is "Constitutional Monarchy."

REPUBLIC

A government where people elect representatives
bound by a constitution.

Hello Mr. Fox

I need a new family.
How do you make
the rules in your family?

We pick a leader who leads the pack.
I believe humans call that a "Republic."

DICTATOR

A government with an absolute, totalitarian ruler.

Hello Mr. Oak

How do you make
the rules in your family?

I do not think you will like my system.
It is fun for me because I take most of
the sunlight in the day and nutrition
from the soil. Only small plants survive here.
I am a dictator. In addition, I am totalitarian.
I dominate everything in my kingdom.

THEOCRACY

Where decisions are dictated by a chosen religion.

ARISTOCRACY

Governance is assigned to a privileged class who believe

that the elite know better than the common man.

Now remember this young man.

Aristocracy is rule by the nobles.

Theocracy is rule by a religious authority.

OLIGARCHY

Government where power is held by an elite few.

Hi little fish

How do you make
The rules in your family?

Well I do not have any say in the rules.
A few of the powerful fish make all the rules.
That is Oligarchy

COMMUNISM

A single party government that owns all Means of Production

DEMOCRACY

Representative Democracy: Citizens elect public office holders to conduct government affairs.

Hey Zephyr – Check out how we operate. We choose a leader to lead us in flight and we work as a team. Our leader will lead us in a v-formation so all the trailing birds can be guided easily. The other experienced birds support the team by honking instructions. When the leader is tired, it signals to another bird to take over his spot.

So it's not about who makes the rules – it's about our collective goals. I suppose that is what you would call "Democracy."

Printed in the United States
By Bookmasters